The Unbreakable Brain Book of Mastering Your Mind:

The Ultimate Cognitive Behavioral Therapy Handbook

Table of Contents

Understanding the Power of Cognitive Behavioral Therapy 8

Chapter 1: Foundations of CBT 13

    What is Cognitive Behavioral Therapy? ... 13

    Historical Development and Key Figures 15

    The Cognitive Triangle: Thoughts, Feelings, Behaviors 19

Chapter 2: The Unbreakable Mindset 23

    Cultivating a Resilient and Positive Mindset 23

    Identifying and Challenging Negative Thought Patterns 27

    Introduction to Cognitive Restructuring . 31

Chapter 3: Emotions and Beliefs 35

Emotion Regulation Techniques 35

Examining Core Beliefs and Their Influence..............................39

Cognitive Distortions: Unmasking Unhelpful Thinking..........................43

Chapter 4: Mastering Behavioral Change ...47

Behavior Analysis: Understanding Your Actions..............................47

Setting SMART Goals for Lasting Change .50

Behavioral Experiments: Testing New Approaches......................................54

Chapter 5: Overcoming Anxiety and Fear ...58

Understanding Anxiety and Its Triggers..58

Exposure Therapy: Facing Your Fears......62

Relaxation Techniques and Stress Management 66

Chapter 6: Breaking Free from Depression 71

Recognizing the Patterns of Depression .. 71

Behavioral Activation: Finding Pleasure and Meaning 75

Cognitive Strategies for Managing Depressive Symptoms 79

Chapter 7: Strengthening Relationships 84

Communication Skills: Building Healthy Connections 84

Addressing Conflict and Misunderstandings 88

Social Anxiety and Building Social Confidence 93

Chapter 8: Self-Care and Well-Being............98

The Role of Self-Care in Mental Health......98

Practicing Mindfulness and Grounding Techniques......................102

Building a Sustainable Self-Care Routine 105

Chapter 9: Maintaining Progress and Relapse Prevention..........................110

Strategies for Maintaining Positive Changes............................110

Recognizing Warning Signs of Relapse..114

Creating a Personalized Relapse Prevention Plan..............................119

Chapter 10: Your Unbreakable Future......124

Reflecting on Your CBT Journey..............124

Applying CBT Principles Beyond the Book 128

Understanding the Power of Cognitive Behavioral Therapy

Cognitive Behavioral Therapy (CBT) is a popular and effective type of psychotherapy that focuses on the interaction of thoughts, feelings, and behaviors. It is based on the premise that our perceptions and interpretations of situations have a significant impact on our emotional responses and actions. CBT was developed in the 1960s by Aaron T. Beck and has since become one of the most thoroughly investigated and performed therapeutic techniques.

Key Principles of CBT:

1. ***Cognitive Restructuring:*** CBT focuses on recognizing and overcoming negative or distorted cognitive processes. These ideas, known as "cognitive distortions," can exacerbate emotional suffering. Individuals can adjust their emotional reactions by recognizing these distortions and replacing them with more balanced and accurate thinking.

2. **Behavioral Activation:** This principle focuses on boosting participation in good and rewarding activities, even when someone is feeling down or unmotivated. Individuals can break the cycle of depression and anxiety by engaging in fun and gratifying activities.

3. **Exposure Therapy:** Exposure therapy, which is commonly used to treat anxiety disorders, includes gradually and carefully addressing fearful events or items. People learn that their anxiety lessens with repeated exposure, allowing them to form new, healthy connections with formerly anxiety-inducing stimuli.

4. **Skill Building:** CBT teaches people coping methods and problem-solving abilities to help them deal with difficult situations. These abilities may include, among other things, assertiveness training, stress management strategies, and communication skills.

5. **Homework and Practice:** CBT frequently includes homework assignments that urge people to apply what they learn in therapy to real-life situations. This

approach reinforces learning and promotes gradual, long-term development.

6. **Collaborative Approach:** CBT is usually done in a collaborative and structured setting. Therapists assist clients in setting objectives, tracking progress, and developing specialized tactics that are adapted to each individual's needs and skills.

7. **Focus on Present and Future:** While CBT may refer to past experiences, it is primarily concerned with the present and the future. It strives to solve present issues while also developing skills to deal with future concerns.

Applications of CBT:

CBT has been successfully used to treat a wide range of psychological conditions, including:

1. **Depression:** CBT assists people in recognizing and challenging negative thought patterns that contribute to feelings of despair and hopelessness.

2. **Anxiety Disorders:** CBT is beneficial in the treatment of a variety of anxiety disorders, including generalized anxiety disorder, social anxiety disorder, panic disorder, and particular phobias.

3. **Obsessive-Compulsive Disorder (OCD):** A type of CBT known as exposure and response prevention is often used to treat OCD by gradually exposing individuals to their obsessions and avoiding compulsive behaviors.

4. **Post-Traumatic Stress Disorder (PTSD):** CBT, particularly trauma-focused CBT, assists people in processing and coping with traumatic experiences.

5. **Eating Disorders:** In illnesses such as anorexia nervosa, bulimia nervosa, and binge-eating disorder, CBT can treat distorted body image and harmful eating practices.

6. **Substance Use Disorders:** CBT is frequently used in addiction treatment programs to address the

underlying ideas and behaviors that lead to substance misuse.

7. **_Insomnia:_** CBT for insomnia focuses on building healthy sleep patterns, enhancing sleep hygiene, and resolving sleep-related anxiety.

8. **_Anger Management:_** CBT strategies can help people regulate their anger by recognizing triggers, changing mental patterns, and teaching effective communication skills.

Individual or group therapy sessions are commonly used to administer CBT, although it can also be adapted for internet platforms and self-help resources. Because CBT is collaborative in nature, individuals can actively participate in their own recovery process and learn vital skills for long-term mental health management. While CBT is highly beneficial for many people, different people may respond better to various therapeutic approaches, and a skilled mental health practitioner can assist select the most appropriate treatment plan.

Chapter 1: Foundations of CBT

What is Cognitive Behavioral Therapy?

Cognitive Behavioral Therapy (CBT) is a popular psychotherapy technique that focuses on the relationship between thoughts, feelings, and behaviors. It is a goal-oriented and evidence-based type of treatment that tries to assist individuals in identifying and changing patterns of thinking and behavior that contribute to emotional discomfort, mental health concerns, and problematic behaviors.

CBT is based on the notion that our thoughts, emotions, and behaviors are all interconnected and can impact one another. Negative or distorted thought patterns can lead to emotional suffering and undesirable actions, as well as the other way around. CBT aims to interrupt these cycles by assisting individuals in becoming more aware of their thought patterns, challenging unreasonable or counterproductive ideas, and developing more adaptive ways of thinking and responding to events.

CBT typically involves the following components:

1. ***Cognitive Restructuring:*** Identifying and addressing negative or distorted thought patterns (cognitive distortions) that contribute to emotional suffering is part of this process. Individuals can build more balanced and realistic attitudes by evaluating the evidence for and against these ideas.

2. ***Behavioral Activation:*** This component focuses on recognizing and changing habits that contribute to or maintain mental health problems. People learn to participate in more positive and adaptive actions while decreasing avoidance or withdrawal.

3. ***Skill Building:*** CBT frequently teaches individuals coping skills and emotional management tactics such as relaxation techniques, problem-solving abilities, and communication skills.

4. ***Homework Assignments:*** Individuals are frequently given homework tasks between sessions to practice the skills they've learned in therapy. This aids

in the reinforcement of new patterns of thought and behavior in real-life circumstances.

5. **Collaborative Approach:** CBT is typically a collaborative procedure between the therapist and the individual. They collaborate to define goals, identify challenges, and devise change tactics.

CBT has been thoroughly examined and found to be beneficial in the treatment of a wide range of mental health illnesses, including depression, anxiety disorders, phobias, obsessive-compulsive disorder (OCD), post-traumatic stress disorder (PTSD), and others. It is frequently used either alone or in conjunction with other therapy techniques and drugs.

While CBT is quite helpful for many people, certain people may respond better to different treatment approaches. Consultation with a mental health specialist can assist in determining the best treatment for an individual's specific requirements.

Historical Development and Key Figures

The history of psychology and its significant individuals is a complicated and varied subject, but I can present an outline of some of the field's most prominent figures and notable achievements:

1. **Ancient Philosophers:** Psychology can be traced back to ancient philosophers such as Plato and Aristotle, who studied the mind, perception, and conduct.

2. **Wilhelm Wundt (1832-1920):** Wundt is widely considered to be the father of contemporary psychology. In 1879, he founded the first psychology laboratory in Leipzig, Germany, and his research centered on the scientific study of consciousness through introspection.

3. **William James (1842-1910):** James, an American philosopher and psychologist, wrote "The Principles of Psychology," which is regarded as one of psychology's most significant publications. From a pragmatic

standpoint, he offered notions such as functionalism and the study of consciousness.

4. ***Sigmund Freud (1856-1939):*** Freud is most known for developing psychoanalysis, a mental theory and therapeutic technique that investigates the function of the unconscious mind and the impact of early childhood experiences on behavior.

5. ***John B. Watson (1878-1958):*** Watson is regarded as a founder of behaviorism, a school of thought that stressed the study of observable behavior while dismissing the study of internal mental processes.

6. ***B.F. Skinner (1904-1990):*** Skinner established the theory of operant conditioning, which focuses on the consequences of conduct in influencing future actions, as an extension of behaviorism.

7. ***Jean Piaget (1896-1980):*** Piaget is well-known for his contributions to developmental psychology. He created a cognitive development theory that outlined how children's thinking processes evolve as they mature.

8. ***Carl Rogers (1902-1987):*** Rogers is well-known for his contributions to humanistic psychology, particularly his emphasis on the necessity of self-actualization and the function of the therapist-client connection in therapy.

9. ***Albert Bandura (1925-2021):*** Bandura created social learning theory and the idea of self-efficacy, both of which emphasize the importance of observational learning and one's belief in one's capacity to complete tasks.

10. ***Cognitive Revolution (1950s-1960s):*** This time in psychology saw a change toward a focus on cognitive processes. Aaron T. Beck, who invented cognitive therapy, and Ulric Neisser, who coined the phrase "cognitive psychology," were key leaders in this movement."

11. ***Contemporary Psychology:*** Psychology is still evolving, with numerous disciplines and subfields such as clinical psychology, social psychology, neuropsychology, and others. The field's continued

development has been aided by prominent contemporary leaders and researchers.

These are only a few of the historical figures and developments in the area of psychology. It's worth noting that psychology is a dynamic and diverse science, with multiple schools of thought and continuing research that change our understanding of the human mind and behavior.

The Cognitive Triangle: Thoughts, Feelings, Behaviors

The Cognitive Triangle, commonly referred to as the Cognitive Triad, is a core concept in cognitive psychology and Cognitive Behavioral Therapy (CBT). It emphasizes the interdependence of three important elements: thoughts, feelings (emotions), and behaviors. Understanding this triangle can help us understand how these factors influence and interact with one another, shaping our overall experiences and well-being.

Here's a breakdown of each component of the Cognitive Triangle:

1. ***Thoughts:*** The beliefs, interpretations, and impressions we have about ourselves, others, and the world around us are referred to as thoughts. These can be conscious or unconscious, and they influence how we process information and make meaning of our experiences. Thoughts might be reasonable, twisted, negative, or positive, automatic, or intentional. The Cognitive Triangle views ideas as a major aspect that controls both emotions and behaviors.

2. ***Feelings (Emotions):*** Our emotional reactions to events, situations, and thoughts are referred to as emotions. They can range from love and happiness to despair, fear, and fury, among other emotions. feelings are inextricably tied to our thinking, since our perceptions of events influence the feelings we feel. For example, if we evaluate a situation as dangerous, we may experience fear or anxiety.

3. ***Behaviors:*** The activities and reactions we engage in as a result of our thoughts and emotions are referred to as behaviors. These can be obvious activities, such as what we say or do, or more subtle behaviors, such as avoiding particular circumstances or procrastinating.

Our thoughts and emotions drive our behaviors, which in turn influence how we feel and think.

The Cognitive Triangle illustrates how these three elements are interconnected and mutually influence each other. Here's an example of how it might work:

Scenario: Assume you're about to deliver a presentation at work.

- **Thoughts:** "I'm not prepared for this presentation," you think. I'm going to screw up."

- **Feelings:** Anxiety and anxiousness are triggered by these ideas.

- **Behaviors:** You may start fidgeting, have a beating heart, or become sweating as a result of your worried feelings.

In this case, negative ideas about the presentation caused anxiety, which showed as bodily and behavioral responses.

CBT employs the Cognitive Triangle to assist people in identifying and challenging unhelpful or distorted thoughts, resulting in changes in feelings and behaviors. Individuals can learn to reframe their thoughts, manage their emotions, and participate in more adaptive behaviors by identifying the links between these components, thereby enhancing their mental health and general well-being.

Overall, the Cognitive Triangle is an effective tool for comprehending the intricate relationships between thoughts, feelings, and behaviors and how these influence our psychological experiences.

Chapter 2: The Unbreakable Mindset

Cultivating a Resilient and Positive Mindset

Maintaining mental well-being and efficiently navigating life's adversities requires cultivating a resilient and happy mindset. Here are some techniques to help you cultivate such a mindset:

1. ***Practice Self-Awareness:*** Begin by becoming more conscious of your own thoughts, feelings, and reactions. Pay attention to any negative thought patterns or self-limiting ideas that may be preventing you from moving forward.

2. ***Challenge Negative Thoughts:*** Take a step back when you catch yourself thinking badly and question those thoughts. Consider whether there is data to back them up or whether you are creating assumptions. Look for more fair and realistic viewpoints.

3. ***Cultivate Optimism:*** Concentrate on the good features of a situation. Recognize the things you're grateful for to practice gratitude. Optimism does not imply ignoring obstacles; rather, it involves having a positive attitude in the face of adversity.

4. ***Practice Mindfulness:*** Being mindful entails being present in the moment without judgment. It can help you handle stress and become more aware of your thoughts and emotions. Regular mindfulness meditation or deep breathing exercises can be beneficial.

5. ***Build Resilience:*** The ability to recover from hardship is referred to as resilience. Develop coping strategies, problem-solving skills, and a solid support network. Remember that setbacks are a part of life, and your reaction is important.

6. ***Set Realistic Goals:*** Setting attainable goals gives you a sense of purpose and direction. To prevent feeling overwhelmed, divide larger goals into smaller, more achievable steps.

7. ***Focus on Growth:*** Accept challenges as opportunities for development. Consider failures to be learning opportunities that can help you improve and learn new abilities.

8. ***Practice Self-Compassion:*** Treat yourself with the same compassion and understanding that you would extend to a friend. When things don't go as planned, don't be too hard on yourself.

9. ***Surround Yourself with Positivity:*** Surround yourself with individuals who bring you up. Reduce your exposure to negativity, whether through harmful relationships, the news, or social media.

10. ***Engage in Physical Activity:*** Regular exercise has numerous physical and mental health advantages. It produces endorphins, which are natural mood enhancers.

11. ***Practice Gratitude:*** Take some time each day to think about what you're grateful for. This technique can

help you shift your emphasis to optimism and improve your general well-being.

12. **Engage in Hobbies:** Activities that you enjoy can bring a sense of accomplishment as well as relaxation. Hobbies provide additional possibilities to learn and improve.

13. **Learn from Mistakes:** Instead than concentrating on mistakes, turn them into stepping stones for growth. Adopt a growth mentality that prioritizes learning and progress.

14. **Limit Negative Self-Talk:** Positive affirmations and loving self-talk should be used instead of self-critical or self-defeating language.

15. **Seek Professional Help:** If you're having trouble keeping an optimistic attitude or dealing with major issues, consider obtaining help from a therapist or counselor.

Keep in mind that developing a resilient and happy mindset requires time and practice. Be gentle with yourself and use these tactics consistently to gradually shift your viewpoint and overall well-being.

Identifying and Challenging Negative Thought Patterns

Identifying and addressing negative thinking patterns is a core skill in cognitive behavioral therapy (CBT) and can make a significant difference in your mental health. Here's a step-by-step strategy to identifying and addressing these negative thought patterns:

1. *Self-Awareness:* Begin by observing your thoughts throughout the day. Recognize when you are anxious, upset, or depressed. Attempt to identify the thoughts that accompany these experiences.

2. *Record Your Thoughts:* To record negative ideas, keep a thinking journal or utilize a note-taking tool. Make a note of the scenario, your thoughts, emotions, and any following behaviors.

3. *Categorize Negative Thought Patterns:* Determine the most common negative thought processes. These patterns are frequently classified as follows:

- **Catastrophizing:** preparing for the worst-case scenario.

- **All-or-Nothing Thinking:** Seeing problems in black-and-white terms, without taking into account the gray area.

- **Personalization:** blaming oneself for situations over which you have no control.

- **Mind Reading:** Assuming you know what other people are thinking, generally negatively.

- **Filtering:** Neglecting the positive features of a situation in order to focus solely on the negative.

- **Overgeneralization:** Using a single unpleasant occurrence to draw widespread negative implications.

4. Gather Evidence: Once you've recognized a negative thought, confront it with data that both supports and opposes it. Consider whether your concept has a factual basis or whether you're creating assumptions.

5. Ask Critical Questions: Start a conversation with yourself to challenge your negative thought habits. Consider the following queries:

- *Is this viewpoint supported by facts or assumptions?*

- *What could possibly go wrong? What is the likelihood?*

- *Is my perspective on the situation all-or-nothing?*

- *Have I been in similar circumstances before, and how did they work out?*

- *Would a trusted friend or colleague have the same thought in this situation?*

- **What is another, more balanced perspective on this situation?**

6. Reframe and Generate Balanced Thoughts: Work on reframing your negative thought with a more balanced and realistic one after gathering data and addressing key questions. Consider alternative interpretations and positive aspects of the circumstance.

7. Practice and Repetition: Changing negative thought habits takes time and practice. This procedure will grow more natural and efficient over time.

8. Use Affirmations and Positive Self-Talk: Create affirmations to fight your negative thought habits. Replace self-critical or negative self-talk with these affirmations.

9. Monitor Progress: Review your thinking notebook on a regular basis to keep track of your development. Recognize patterns of improvement and appreciate your victories.

10. Seek Professional Help: Consider obtaining help from a therapist or counselor if negative thought patterns are firmly rooted or have a substantial influence on your well-being. They can offer advice and extra techniques geared to your individual need.

Be patient with yourself because altering thought habits takes time and effort. Identifying and addressing negative thoughts gradually might lead to a more balanced and happy attitude on life.

Introduction to Cognitive Restructuring

Cognitive restructuring is a cognitive behavioral therapy (CBT) strategy that focuses on recognizing, confronting, and changing negative or unreasonable thought processes. Cognitive restructuring aims to help people create more balanced, realistic, and adaptive ways of thinking, which leads to better emotional well-being and behavior.

Cognitive restructuring acknowledges the intimate relationship that exists between our thoughts, emotions, and behaviors. It is based on the notion that the way we interpret and experience events, rather than the events themselves, influences our emotional reactions and behaviors. We can alter our emotional responses and reactions by modifying our interpretations.

Here's an overview of how cognitive restructuring works:

1. ***Identification of Negative Thoughts:*** Identifying negative thought patterns that contribute to emotional pain or problematic behavior is the first step in cognitive restructuring. These are often automatic ideas that are not entirely conscious.

2. ***Examination of Evidence:*** Individuals are urged to analyze the information that supports and contradicts their negative thoughts once they have identified them. This contributes to a more balanced view of the situation.

3. ***Challenging Cognitive Distortions:*** Cognitive distortions are illogical or incorrect methods of thinking

that can lead to undesirable feelings. All-or-nothing thinking, catastrophizing, overgeneralization, personalizing, and other distortions are examples of this. Individuals learn to notice and resist these distortions through cognitive restructuring.

4. **Generating Alternative Thoughts:** Individuals focus on producing alternative thoughts that are more balanced and realistic after challenging distortions. These new ideas take a larger view of the situation into consideration.

5. **Behavioral Experiments:** Individuals may sometimes conduct behavioral experiments to test the veracity of their negative ideas. These experiments provide empirical data to refute illogical ideas.

6. **Practice and Repetition:** Changing mental patterns is a skill that takes time and effort. Participating in cognitive restructuring exercises on a regular basis helps to reinforce new ways of thinking.

7. **Integration with Emotion and Behavior:** Emotions and behaviors frequently accompany changes

in cognitive processes. Individuals can experience more pleasant emotional states and engage in healthier actions by addressing the source of bad emotions (negative thoughts).

8. **Long-Term Impact:** Cognitive restructuring can lead to a shift in overall cognitive habits over time, resulting in a more resilient and happy mindset.

In the context of therapy, cognitive restructuring is a collaborative process between the individual and the therapist. Individuals can, however, learn and practice cognitive restructuring strategies on their own, especially after comprehending the fundamental ideas.

Remember that cognitive restructuring does not eradicate all negative thoughts, but it does allow people to manage and respond to them in a healthier way. If you want to learn more about cognitive restructuring, talk to a mental health professional who specializes in CBT or cognitive therapy.

Chapter 3: Emotions and Beliefs

Emotion Regulation Techniques

Emotion regulation techniques are tactics and abilities that assist people in managing and coping with their emotions in a healthy and adaptable manner. Emotions are a normal aspect of the human experience, but being able to control them well can improve mental health and general life pleasure. Here are some approaches for emotion management to consider:

1. ***Mindfulness Meditation:*** Being totally present in the moment without judgment is what mindfulness entails. Mindfulness meditation activities can assist you in becoming more aware of your emotions as they arise, allowing you to observe them without reacting instantly. This awareness has the potential to lead to more careful and balanced reactions.

2. ***Deep Breathing:*** Deep breathing techniques, such as diaphragmatic breathing, can assist to reduce stress in the body. Taking calm, deep breaths activates the

relaxation response in the body, which can assist manage powerful emotions.

3. **Progressive Muscle Relaxation:** This technique entails systematically tensing and relaxing various muscle groups throughout the body. It can help alleviate physical tension caused by stress and anxiety while also providing a sensation of serenity.

4. **Grounding Techniques:** To return your attention back to the present moment, grounding techniques involve focusing on your immediate surroundings. You can, for example, describe what you see, feel distinct textures, or listen to specific noises.

5. **Self-Compassion:** When dealing with challenging emotions, be gentle and understanding to yourself. Use self-compassionate self-talk and treat yourself like a helpful friend.

6. **Emotion Labeling:** Simply naming and acknowledging your feelings can help to relax the brain. Say to yourself, "I'm feeling anxious," rather than avoiding or denying the experience.

7. **_Distraction:_** Engage in tasks that will briefly divert your attention away from your powerful feelings. This can involve reading, watching a movie, participating in a hobby, or spending time with family and friends.

8. **_Problem-Solving:_** If your emotions are linked to a specific situation, problem-solving approaches can assist you in addressing the issue and reducing emotional suffering.

9. **_Journaling:_** Keep a journal to record your feelings and thoughts. This can help you understand patterns, process emotions, and give a healthy avenue for expression.

10. **_Social Support:_** Talking about your feelings with friends, family, or a therapist can bring affirmation, comfort, and new views.

11. **_Positive Activities:_** Take part in things that bring you delight, such as going for a stroll, listening to music, or pursuing a creative endeavor. Positive experiences can help to balance out bad emotions.

12. **_Cognitive Reframing:_** Negative or illogical thoughts that contribute to intense emotions should be challenged. Replace them with more realistic and balanced thinking.

13. **_Limit Stressors:_** Determine and handle stressors in your life. Reducing unneeded stress can help to keep unpleasant feelings at bay.

14. **_Healthy Lifestyle:_** Regular exercise, balanced eating, adequate sleep, and avoiding excessive substance use can all have a favorable impact on your emotional state.

Remember that not every strategy will work equally well for everyone, and it's fine to try several things to see what works best for you. Developing a variety of emotion regulation abilities can give you with a toolkit for managing your emotions in a variety of scenarios. If your emotions are constantly overwhelming or interfering with your daily life, consult with a mental health expert.

Examining Core Beliefs and Their Influence

Individuals' core beliefs are deeply embedded views or assumptions about themselves, others, and the world around them. These ideas are frequently developed early in life and can have a substantial impact on thoughts, emotions, and behaviors. Examining and comprehending core beliefs is an important component of cognitive therapy and cognitive behavioral therapy (CBT), as these beliefs can contribute to both emotional suffering and maladaptive behavior. This is how basic beliefs are examined:

1. *Identifying Core Beliefs:* Begin by noticing and understanding the core concepts that are at work in your life. These assumptions are frequently automatic and may not be immediately apparent. Core beliefs are more basic and all-encompassing than specific thoughts you may have in a certain situation.

2. *Examples of Core Beliefs:* Core beliefs can be positive, negative, or a combination of the two. Here are several examples:

- " I'm unlovable."

- " I am knowledgeable and capable."

- " Others are constantly plotting to harm me."

- " The world is a secure environment."

3. *Tracing Origins:* Investigate the origins of these key beliefs. They are frequently the result of early experiences, family dynamics, cultural influences, or big life events.

4. *Understanding Influence:* Core beliefs serve as interpretive filters for events, situations, and relationships. They have an impact on our ideas, feelings, and behaviors. For example, if someone has a basic belief that they are unlovable, each rejection may be interpreted as proof that their belief is correct.

5. *Identifying Cognitive Distortions:* Cognitive distortions—irrational and biased methods of thinking—are frequently related with core beliefs. All-or-nothing thinking, emotive reasoning, leaping to conclusions, and personalizing are examples of common distortions.

6. Challenging Core Beliefs: You can begin to confront and review these beliefs once you've recognized a fundamental belief and the cognitive distortions associated with it. Consider the following:

- "What evidence supports or contradicts this belief?"

- " Are there any other explanations for the events that support this belief?"

- " What would another person, such as a friend, think about this situation?"

7. Replacing with Balanced Beliefs: Replace the rigid and extreme basic beliefs with more balanced and realistic views. These new beliefs consider a larger perspective and include data from various perspectives.

8. Behavioral Experiments: Conduct behavioral experiments to validate your key assumptions. Seek out events that test your core beliefs and keep track of the outcomes.

9. *Cognitive Restructuring:* Thought recordings and addressing cognitive distortions are common cognitive restructuring approaches used to transform basic beliefs and replace them with more adaptive alternatives.

10. *Gradual Change:* It takes time and effort to change underlying ideas. You can gradually move from habitual, negative thought patterns to more balanced and constructive ways of thinking with effort and repetition.

Working with a CBT-trained therapist or counselor can be especially beneficial when it comes to exploring and addressing underlying beliefs. A expert can assist you navigate the process, provide insights, and devise successful ways for changing these deeply embedded ideas.

Cognitive Distortions: Unmasking Unhelpful Thinking

Cognitive distortions are faulty or biased methods of thinking that can lead to negative emotions, maladaptive behaviors, and mistaken perceptions of reality. They are also known as thinking traps or irrational thought patterns. Recognizing and removing these distortions is an important step in cognitive behavioral therapy (CBT) and other types of psychological well-being interventions. Here are some instances of common cognitive distortions:

1. **All-or-Nothing Thinking (Black-and-White Thinking):** Seeing things in extremes without regard for the intermediate ground or complexity. "I'm a complete failure if I don't get this promotion," for example.

2. **Overgeneralization:** Using isolated occurrences to draw larger conclusions. "I made a mistake on this project," for example. I usually botch things up.

3. ***Mental Filtering (Selective Abstraction):*** Neglecting the positive parts of a situation in order to focus solely on the negative. For instance, "I received positive feedback on my presentation, but I can't stop thinking about the one person who seemed uninterested."

4. ***Discounting the Positive:*** Positive experiences or attributes are minimized or dismissed as trivial or irrelevant. "I aced the exam, but it was just a simple test that anyone could have passed," for example.

5. ***Jumping to Conclusions:*** Conclusions drawn without sufficient proof.

- ***Mind Reading:*** Assuming you are aware of what others are thinking. "My friend hasn't texted me back; they must be upset with me," for example.

- ***Fortune Telling:*** Predicting unfavorable events without any basis in fact. For instance, "I'm going to fail the interview; they'll never hire me."

6. ***Magnification and Minimization (Catastrophizing and Trivializing):*** Exaggerating the importance of unpleasant events while downplaying the significance of favorable ones. "I made a mistake at work; my boss is going to fire me for sure."

7. ***Emotional Reasoning:*** Believing that just because you feel something, it must be true. "I'm so worried about this situation; it must be dangerous," for example.

8. ***Should Statements:*** Having unrealistic and strict expectations of oneself and others. "I should always be productive," for example. I shouldn't require breaks.

9. ***Personalization:*** Blaming yourself for events over which you have no control. "My partner is in a bad mood; it must be because of something I did."

10. ***Labeling and Mislabeling:*** Applying unduly unfavorable labels to oneself or others based on isolated behaviour. "I made a mistake; I'm a total failure."

11. ***Catastrophizing:*** Predicting the worst-case scenario of a circumstance. "If I don't get this job, my entire career will be ruined," for example.

Recognizing and addressing cognitive distortions through strategies such as cognitive restructuring might help you build more balanced and realistic ways of thinking. You may improve your emotional well-being, decision-making, and overall perspective of the world around you by uncovering these problematic thought patterns. If you find that these distortions are causing you significant distress, seeing a CBT-trained mental health professional can provide direction and assistance.

Chapter 4: Mastering Behavioral Change

Behavior Analysis: Understanding Your Actions

In psychology, behavior analysis is a systematic technique to understanding and evaluating human behavior. It entails investigating the connections between actions, antecedents (events that occur before behaviors), and consequences (events that occur after acts). Individuals might get insights on why they participate in specific behaviors and how to adjust them to attain desired outcomes by evaluating these encounters. The following is how behavior analysis works:

1. Define the Behavior: Begin by outlining the behavior you wish to study. Be explicit and impartial when expressing the behavior you're looking for.

2. Identify Antecedents: An antecedent is an occurrence or scenario that occurs immediately before an action. They have the ability to either trigger or impact behavior. Determine what occurs immediately before the activity under consideration.

3. Analyze Consequences: Consequences are the results or occurrences that occur as a result of a conduct. They can impact whether the conduct will occur again in the future. Examine the consequences of the conduct, such as any incentives, penalties, or results.

4. Patterns and Functions: Look for patterns in the relationship between antecedents and consequences and behavior. Consider the behavior's function—what purpose it provides for the individual. Behaviors can be used to garner attention, escape from a situation, seek sensory stimulation, or acquire access to desired goods.

5. Positive Reinforcement: Positive reinforcement is rewarding or offering pleasant consequences after a behavior to improve the chance of that behavior occurring again. Determine whether positive reinforcement is involved in the behavior's persistence.

6. Negative Reinforcement: Determine whether negative reinforcement is impacting the behavior by eliminating or avoiding something unpleasant after a behavior, which also raises the chance of the behavior occurring again.

7. Punishment: Punishment entails giving an adverse consequence after a conduct to reduce its likelihood. Determine whether punishment has an effect on behavior.

8. Functional Assessment: A functional assessment may be necessary for more complicated activities. This is collecting information about the antecedents, behaviors, and effects in numerous scenarios in order to identify patterns and functions.

9. Behavior Modification: You might examine ways to modify the behavior after you have a better knowledge of its antecedents and repercussions. This could entail offering positive reinforcement for desired behaviors, altering antecedents to lessen triggers, or implementing techniques to deal with negative consequences.

10. Track Progress: Monitor the behavior and its relationships with antecedents and consequences on an ongoing basis. Keep track of behavioral changes and the effectiveness of treatments you've put in place.

Behavior analysis is widely employed in a variety of situations, such as clinical therapy, education, and organizational behavior management. It assists individuals in gaining insight into their activities, making educated decisions regarding behavior modification, and developing effective methods for accomplishing their objectives. If you're suffering with a behavior you'd like to change, speaking with a behavior analyst or a mental health expert can help.

Setting SMART Goals for Lasting Change

Setting SMART objectives is a smart strategy to achieve meaningful and long-term change in your life. Specific, Measurable, Achievable, Relevant, and Time-Bound is an acronym that stands for Specific, Measurable, Achievable, Relevant, and Time-Bound. You may design goals that are well-defined, practical, and actionable if you follow these criteria. Here's how to develop SMART goals for long-term success:

1. **Specific (S):** Your objective should be clear and specific, with no space for ambiguity.

- Ask yourself, "What exactly do I want to accomplish?" What makes this objective so essential to me?

   For instance, "I want to improve my physical fitness by jogging regularly."

2. **Measurable (M):** Your objective should have a measurable mechanism to track progress and determine when you've met it.

- Consider how you will track your success. What are the success indicators?

   "I'll jog for 30 minutes three times a week."

3. **Achievable (A):** Given your present resources, talents, and limits, your aim should be realistic and attainable.

- Is it possible for you to achieve this goal? Do I have the resources to complete it?

  "Given my current schedule, I am able to commit to jogging in the mornings."

4. **Relevant (R):** Your target should be consistent with your values and long-term objectives.

- Consider whether this aim is consistent with your overall goals and aspirations?

  "Improving my physical fitness aligns with my desire to live a healthier lifestyle," for example.

5. **Time-Bound (T):** Your goal should have a deadline for completion, creating a sense of urgency.

- Consider when you want to reach this aim. What is a reasonable time frame?

  "I will jog for 30 minutes three times a week for the next three months," for example.

When these factors are combined, the SMART goal is: "I want to improve my physical fitness by jogging for 30 minutes three times a week in the mornings for the next three months."

Additional Tips:

- Divide larger objectives into smaller, more achievable tasks.

- To stay motivated, write down your SMART goals and keep them visible.

- Continuously monitor your progress and change your strategy as needed.

- Celebrate your accomplishments along the way to keep yourself motivated.

Setting SMART objectives gives you a clear roadmap for making great and long-term improvements in your life. Whether you want to improve your health, your work, your relationships, or your personal growth, the SMART criteria can help you stay organized, motivated, and ultimately successful.

Behavioral Experiments: Testing New Approaches

Cognitive behavioral therapy (CBT) relies heavily on behavioral experiments. They entail actively experimenting with new ideas or behaviors in order to confront and transform harmful beliefs, assumptions, or cognitive distortions. Individuals can use these experiments to obtain real-world evidence to assess the veracity of their opinions and beliefs. Here's how to run effective behavioral experiments:

1. ***Identify the Belief or Assumption:*** Begin by determining the specific idea or assumption to be tested. This should be a thinking or belief that causes emotional suffering, avoidance, or undesirable conduct.

2. ***Formulate a Hypothesis:*** Create a hypothesis about what you expect to happen when you challenge the belief or assumption. What do you think the experiment's outcome will be?

3. ***Design the Experiment:*** Plan the experiment's specifics. Determine what actions or behaviors you will

do to refute the belief. Make certain that the experiment is explicit, measurable, and practicable.

4. **Set Clear Goals:** Define the experiment's goals or objectives. What are you hoping to gain or learn from this experiment? Determine what success entails.

5. **Execute the Experiment:** Participate actively in the experiment, adhering to the plan you've devised. This could entail exposing yourself to situations that activate the belief or experimenting with new behaviors.

6. **Observe and Document:** Take note of your thoughts, feelings, and behaviors both during and after the experiment. Keep a notebook or take notes to capture your experience.

7. **Evaluate the Results:** Contrast the actual results of the experiment with your original hypothesis. Did the findings support or refute your hypothesis? Be objective and open to the information you've gathered.

8. **Learn and Adjust:** Consider what you learned from the experiment. If the findings contradict your prior

view, explore how you may incorporate this new knowledge into your thinking and behavior.

9. **Repeat as Needed:** To cement new ideas and behaviors, behavioral tests may need to be repeated or adjusted. Don't be disheartened if one trial fails to generate the intended result.

10. **Seek Professional Guidance:** Behavioral tests can be emotionally draining, especially when confronted with deeply held views. If you're struggling or feeling overwhelmed, it's critical to seek the advice and assistance of a skilled CBT therapist.

Example of a Behavioral Experiment:

Belief: "I am unlikable, and people don't want to be around me."

Hypothesis: If I strike up a discussion with a coworker, they will reply positively, and we will have a pleasant exchange.

Experiment: Approach a coworker and strike up a conversation about anything unrelated.

Observations: The coworker answered pleasantly and appeared to be interested in the conversation. They grinned and struck up additional chats on subsequent times.

Evaluation: The findings countered your initial notion that you are unlikable, presenting information that calls your negative self-perception into question.

Behavioral experiments are an effective tool in CBT for challenging and changing negative thought habits. They allow people to learn practical, real-world insights while gradually developing more accurate and adaptive ideas about themselves and their interactions with others.

Chapter 5: Overcoming Anxiety and Fear

Understanding Anxiety and Its Triggers

Anxiety is a normal and healthy reaction to stress or imagined threats. It is uncertainty, worry, or fear regarding upcoming events or situations. While some anxiety is natural, severe or persistent anxiety can be troublesome and impair daily functioning. Understanding anxiety and its triggers is critical for controlling and coping with this emotional response effectively. Here's a quick rundown:

Types of Anxiety:

1. ***Generalized Anxiety Disorder (GAD):*** Excessive and uncontrollable anxiety about numerous parts of life, even when no imminent threat exists.

2. ***Social Anxiety Disorder:*** terror of being evaluated or humiliated causes severe terror and avoidance of social interactions.

3. **_Panic Disorder:_** Characterized by repeated and unexpected panic attacks, which are moments of acute dread followed by physical symptoms such as rapid heartbeat and shortness of breath.

4. **_Specific Phobias:_** Fear of a specific thing or situation, which leads to avoidance behavior.

5. **_Obsessive-Compulsive Disorder (OCD):_** Involves unpleasant, intrusive thoughts (obsessions) and repetitive behavioral or mental acts (compulsions) aimed at alleviating anxiety.

6. **_Post-Traumatic Stress Disorder (PTSD):_** Develops following a stressful experience, resulting in symptoms such as intrusive recollections, avoidance, and heightened arousal.

Common Anxiety Triggers:

1. **_Stressful Life Events:_** Anxiety can be triggered by major life changes such as moving, changing jobs, or experiencing a loss.

2. ***Uncertainty:*** Anxiety can be caused by not knowing the result of a situation or a lack of control.

3. ***Social Situations:*** Interacting with others or being in social situations can cause anxiety in persons who suffer from social anxiety.

4. ***Performance Pressure:*** Performance anxiety can arise when presenting, performing, or being judged in front of others.

5. ***Health Concerns:*** Physical health concerns, illnesses, or symptoms can all contribute to health-related anxiety.

6. ***Catastrophic Thinking:*** Anticipating the worst-case scenario in a variety of situations can exacerbate anxiety.

7. ***Negative Self-Talk:*** Self-criticism and negative thought patterns can aggravate anxiety.

8. **Traumatic Memories:** Recalling traumatic experiences or memories can cause anxiety, especially in people suffering from PTSD.

9. **Phobic Triggers:** Specific phobia-related objects or circumstances might induce extreme anxiety.

10. **Environmental Factors:** Certain surroundings, sounds, or sensory stimuli might cause anxiety in sensitive people.

Coping Strategies for Anxiety:

1. **Deep Breathing and Relaxation Techniques:** Deep breathing, gradual muscle relaxation, or mindfulness can all be used to quiet the body's stress reaction.

2. **Cognitive Restructuring:** Negative thought patterns that contribute to anxiety should be challenged and reframed.

3. **_Exposure Therapy:_** Face anxiety triggers gradually to lessen avoidance and desensitize the fear reaction.

4. **_Physical Activity:_** Exercise can help reduce anxiety by generating endorphins and decreasing stress chemicals.

5. **_Social Support:_** Discuss your feelings and experiences with friends, family, or a therapist.

6. **_Healthy Lifestyle:_** Prioritize adequate sleep, balanced eating, and avoid excessive coffee and alcohol consumption.

7. **_Professional Help:_** If anxiety is interfering with your everyday life, seek help from a mental health professional who can offer useful interventions and solutions.

Understanding anxiety triggers enables you to take proactive efforts to properly manage and cope with your anxiety. If your anxiety is severe or chronic, you should seek professional help to obtain specialized support and therapy.

Exposure Therapy: Facing Your Fears

Exposure therapy is a well-known treatment method for anxiety disorders, phobias, and post-traumatic stress disorder (PTSD). It entails progressively and methodically exposing someone to circumstances, objects, or memories that cause anxiety or terror. Exposure therapy's purpose is to help patients address their fears in a controlled and safe atmosphere, allowing them to realize that their anxiety lessens over time and that their anxieties are frequently unfounded. The following is how exposure therapy works:

1. ***Assessment:*** The therapist and client work together to uncover the precise causes of worry or dread. This could be a circumstance, a thing, a location, or a memory.

2. ***Establishing a Hierarchy:*** Together, the therapist and client develop an anxiety hierarchy, which is a list of scenarios or triggers rated from least to most anxiety-inducing. This hierarchy provides a road plan for exposure.

3. Gradual Exposure: In exposure treatment, the least anxiety-provoking item on the hierarchy is confronted first. The trigger is introduced to the individual in a controlled and systematic manner.

4. Controlled Exposure: There are two main ways to expose yourself:

- **In Vivo Exposure:** In actual life, confronting the feared situation or item.

- **Imaginal Exposure:** Reliving upsetting memories or picturing anxiety-inducing scenarios.

5. Habituation: Individuals often show a diminution in their anxiety reaction after repeated encounters. This is referred to as habituation. It happens because the body and mind become acclimated to the trigger, causing the fear reaction to lessen.

6. Duration and Frequency: The length and frequency of exposure sessions varies according to the individual's progress and tolerance. Sessions may begin briefly and gradually develop in length.

7. Cognitive Restructuring: Individuals have the opportunity to dispute and reframe their negative thoughts and beliefs about the trigger during exposure sessions.

8. Recording Progress: Anxiety levels can be tracked before, during, and after exposure sessions. This helps to indicate the gradual decrease in anxiety.

9. Generalization: As progress is made with one trigger, exposure therapy may be expanded to address similar triggers. This aids in the prevention of avoidance behaviors.

10. Support and Guidance: Exposure therapy is often performed under the supervision of a skilled therapist who gives support, guidance, and anxiety-management measures during the exposure procedure.

11. Maintenance and Relapse Prevention: Individuals are taught coping skills and techniques for long-term anxiety management and relapse prevention.

Exposure therapy can be difficult because it requires confronting fears and concerns on purpose. However, it has been shown to be beneficial in helping people reduce anxiety, minimize avoidance habits, and reclaim control of their life. Working with a skilled therapist who can adjust the approach to your unique requirements and give the necessary support throughout the process is vital if you're considering exposure therapy.

Relaxation Techniques and Stress Management

Relaxation techniques are methods for reducing stress, promoting relaxation, and improving overall well-being. Incorporating these tactics into your routine can help you manage stress, anxiety, and other emotional issues. Here are some excellent stress management and relaxation techniques:

1. Deep Breathing:

- Locate a quiet, comfortable location to sit or lie down.

- Allow your abdomen to lift as you inhale deeply through your nostrils.

- Exhale softly through your lips, relaxing your muscles.

- For many minutes, concentrate on your breath, inhaling and expelling deeply.

2. Progressive Muscle Relaxation:

- Begin with your toes and progress through each muscle group.

- Tend each muscle group for a few seconds, then relax.

- Take note of the contrast between tension and relaxation.

3. Guided Imagery or Visualization:

- Close your eyes and visualize a serene and soothing place.

- Use your imagination to imagine sights, sounds, scents, and textures.

- Spend a few moments immersing yourself in this mental oasis.

4. Mindfulness Meditation:

- Sit comfortably and concentrate on your breath or a particular sensation.

- If your mind wanders, gently bring it back to the present moment.

- Being mindful entails seeing without judgment and being totally present.

5. Progressive Relaxation:

- Relax each muscle group from head to toe, concentrating on releasing tension.

- Begin with your face, neck, and shoulders, working your way down to your feet.

6. Yoga and Stretching:

- To relieve physical tension, practice mild yoga positions or stretches.

- Pay attention to your breathing and the sensations in your body as you move.

7. Aromatherapy:

- To create a relaxing ambiance, use calming scents such as lavender or chamomile.

- To add aroma to the room, use essential oils, candles, or diffusers.

8. Exercise:

- Walking, jogging, or dancing on a regular basis might help reduce stress and enhance mood.

10. Engage in Hobbies:

- Reading, drawing, or gardening, for example, might serve as a kind of relaxation and distraction from pressures.

11. Time Management:

- To avoid feeling overwhelmed, organize your chores and create realistic goals.
- Divide things into smaller, more doable segments.

12. Social Support:

- Spend time with friends and family who can offer emotional support.
- Talking about your feelings and experiences can help you relax.

13. Self-Care:

- Set aside time for self-care activities that bring you joy and relaxation.

- Participate in activities that promote your physical, emotional, and mental well.

Remember that relaxation techniques do not come in one size fits all. It's critical to try out several strategies and see what works best for you. Regular use of these tactics will help you build stress resistance and enhance your capacity to deal with difficult situations. If stress and anxiety are interfering with your daily life, consider seeking help from a mental health expert.

Chapter 6: Breaking Free from Depression

Recognizing the Patterns of Depression

Recognizing depression patterns entails understanding the common indications, symptoms, and behavioral patterns linked with this mood condition. Depression is more than just feeling sad on sometimes; it is a chronic and frequently incapacitating disorder that affects emotions, thoughts, actions, and physical well-being. Here are some crucial patterns to keep an eye out for:

1. Persistent Low Mood:

- Almost every day, I feel gloomy, empty, or hopeless for the majority of the day.

- a loss of interest or pleasure in previously enjoyable activity.

2. Changes in Sleep Patterns:

- Insomnia (inability to fall or stay asleep) or hypersomnia (excessive sleeping).

- Sleep disturbances, such as getting up very early in the morning.

3. Changes in Appetite or Weight:

- Significant weight loss or gain, frequently coupled with appetite fluctuations.

- Loss of appetite or comfort eating.

4. Fatigue and Low Energy:

- Even after rest, you feel physically and mentally exhausted.

- Difficulty starting and finishing work owing to a lack of energy.

5. Feelings of Worthlessness or Guilt:

- Feelings of remorse, worthlessness, or self-blame that are excessive or illogical.

- A perception of being a burden to others.

6. Difficulty Concentrating:

- Reduced concentration, attention, and decision-making abilities.

- Slow thinking and information processing difficulties.

7. Physical Symptoms:

- Physical symptoms that are unexplained, such as headaches, stomach difficulties, or persistent discomfort.

- Medical treatment may not be effective for certain symptoms.

8. Social Withdrawal:

- withholding participation in social events, hobbies, and contact with friends and family.

- Isolation and a sense of being disconnected from people.

9. Suicidal Thoughts:

- Suicide, death, or dying thoughts.

- expressing a wish to end one's life or sentiments of despair about one's future.

10. Irritability and Agitation:

- Unknown cause of irritability, restlessness, or agitation.

- Even minor irritations can elicit strong emotional responses.

11. Loss of Interest:

- Loss of interest in previously enjoyed hobbies, relationships, and activities.

- A general feeling of emptiness and a lack of pleasure.

12. Changes in Self-Care:

- Personal hygiene, grooming, and self-care practices are neglected.

- Feeling too stressed to perform basic everyday tasks.

13. Recurrent Thoughts of Death:

- Frequent thoughts of death or a desire to die.

- The strength of these ideas can range from fleeting to chronic.

It's crucial to remember that everyone's depression experience is unique, and not everyone will exhibit all of these patterns. Depression can also present differently depending on cultural and gender setting. If you or someone you love is suffering from depression, it is critical that you get professional help. A mental health professional, such as a therapist or psychiatrist, can provide an accurate diagnosis, recommend suitable treatment options, and guide you through the recovery process. Depression can be treated, and help is available.

Behavioral Activation: Finding Pleasure and Meaning

Behavioral activation is a treatment strategy used to treat depression that encourages people to engage in more gratifying and meaningful activities. It is founded on the concept that depression frequently results in a decrease in pleasurable and meaningful activities, which can compound emotions of despair and hopelessness. Behavioral activation tries to disrupt this cycle by gradually reintroducing fun and meaningful activities into people's lives. The following is how behavioral activation works:

1. Activity Monitoring:

- Begin by keeping note of your daily activities and rating how much joy or satisfaction each activity provides; this assists in identifying patterns of decreased activity and the relationship between activity levels and mood.

2. Identifying Values and Goals:

- Consider your values, interests, and long-term objectives.
- Identify activities that correspond to these values and goals.

3. Setting Achievable Goals:

- Based on your beliefs and interests, set short and attainable activity objectives.
- Select hobbies that you used to enjoy or new activities that pique your interest.

4. Gradual Exposure:

- Begin with relatively easy tasks and gradually increase the level of difficulty; the idea is to generate a sense of success while avoiding overloading yourself.

5. Scheduling Activities:

- Make an organized daily routine with planned activities; Include a variety of activities that bring pleasure, accomplishment, and social connection.

6. Overcoming Barriers:

- Identify any barriers or negative attitudes that may hinder you from participating in activities.
- Challenge and replace these negative thoughts with cognitive restructuring tools.

7. Tracking Mood Changes:

- Regularly check your mood before and after engaging in activities to understand how activity affects your mood and motivation.

8. Problem-Solving:

- Address any issues that emerge while participating in events.
- Create methods for overcoming barriers and setbacks.

9. Social Interaction:

- Incorporate social activities that entail spending time with friends, family, or support groups. • Social connection helps improve mood.

10. Celebrating Achievements:

- Recognize and appreciate even minor accomplishments; this fosters a sense of accomplishment and boosts self-esteem.

Behavioral activation is intended to progressively break the pattern of avoidance and withdrawal that frequently occurs with depression. Individuals can improve their mood, motivation, and feeling of well-being by actively participating in things that bring them pleasure and significance. While behavioral activation can be done on your own, engaging with a therapist who specializes in this method can offer you with specific advice and support throughout the process.

Cognitive Strategies for Managing Depressive Symptoms

Cognitive techniques can help manage depression symptoms and promote emotional well-being. These tactics are based on cognitive behavioral therapy (CBT), a popular method for treating depression. CBT focuses on recognizing and correcting negative thought processes that contribute to symptoms of depression. Here are some cognitive tactics for dealing with depression symptoms:

1. Cognitive Restructuring:

- Recognize negative and self-critical thoughts that contribute to depression.
- Examine evidence, explore alternate views, and seek more balanced interpretations to challenge and reframe these thoughts.

2. Thought Monitoring:

- Be aware of your thoughts throughout the day.
- Write down any negative or self-critical ideas you have and examine their correctness and impact.

3. ABC Model:

- Use the ABC model to analyze your thoughts:

- A: Activating Event (trigger)

- B: Beliefs (thoughts and interpretations)

- C: Consequences (emotional and behavioral reactions)

- Challenge distorted beliefs (B) to change negative emotional consequences (C).

4. Behavioral Experiments:

- Conduct behavioral experiments to test the accuracy of your negative beliefs.
- Participate in activities that challenge your negative views and acquire evidence to support more balanced viewpoints.

5. Self-Compassion:

- Practice self-compassion by being kind, understanding, and patient with oneself.
- Replace self-criticism with self-acceptance and encouragement.

6. Mindfulness and Meditation:

- Use mindfulness to become more aware of your thoughts and emotions without passing judgment.
- Meditation can help you cultivate present-moment awareness and cultivate a non-reactive attitude toward your ideas.

7. Cognitive Coping Cards:

- Make positive affirmations, coping statements, and realistic viewpoints into cognitive coping cards.
- Use these cards to help you deal with negative ideas.

8. Gratitude Practice:

- Practice thankfulness to focus on the positive things of your life.
- Make a list or keep a journal of things you're grateful for on a regular basis.

9. Reframing Catastrophic Thinking:

- Consider more realistic outcomes to challenge catastrophic thinking (believing the worst-case situation will occur).

- Break huge difficulties down into smaller, more achievable steps.

10. Positive Self-Talk:

- Replace negative self-talk with supportive and encouraging comments.
- Be kind to yourself in the same way you would a friend.

11. Behavioral Activation:

- Participate in activities that provide you joy, accomplishment, and social contact.
- Engage in activities even if you don't feel inspired because they can enhance your mood over time.

12. Setting Realistic Expectations:

- Set realistic goals and expectations for yourself.
- Avoid having unrealistically high expectations, which can lead to emotions of failure.

Remember that putting these cognitive methods into practice requires time and effort. You don't have to execute them all at once; start with the ones that speak to you the most. If you notice that your depression symptoms are interfering with your everyday life, obtaining help from a mental health expert, such as a therapist or psychiatrist, can provide individualized counseling and treatment alternatives.

Chapter 7: Strengthening Relationships

Communication Skills: Building Healthy Connections

Building healthy connections and relationships with people requires effective communication skills. Poor communication can lead to misunderstandings and confrontations, whereas good communication develops understanding, trust, and teamwork. Here are some important communication skills that help you establish and maintain successful relationships:

1. Active Listening:

- Concentrate on the speaker and give them your undivided attention.
- Do not interrupt and do not formulate responses while they are speaking.
- Demonstrate that you are paying attention by nodding, making eye contact, and using vocal cues such as "I see," "I understand," or "Tell me more."

2. Empathy:

- Put yourself in the shoes of the other person and try to comprehend their point of view.
- Recognize their sentiments and emotions, even if you disagree.
- Use sentences such as "I can imagine how you feel" or "That must have been extremely difficult for you."

3. Nonverbal Communication:

- Be aware of your body language, facial expressions, and speech tone.
- Make sure your nonverbal cues match your words and objectives.
- Keep your stance open, make eye contact, and avoid defensive or aggressive movements.

4. Clarity and Conciseness:

- To avoid confusion, express yourself plainly and directly.
- Avoid jargon and unnecessarily complex terms by using plain language.

- Get to the point quickly while offering enough context for comprehension.

5. Asking Open-Ended Questions:

- Use open-ended questions to spark deeper discussions. These questions necessitate more than a yes or no response and can spark interesting debates.

6. Reflective Responding:

- Reflect back what you've heard to demonstrate that you understand and affirm the other person's feelings; this strategy ensures that you've accurately processed their message.

7. Expressing Yourself Assertively:

- Speak plainly and assertively about your views, feelings, and needs.
- Express your feelings using "I" phrases rather than criticizing or accusing others.

8. Avoiding Assumptions:

- When in doubt, clarify facts by asking for explanations or context.
- Avoid assuming what the other person is saying.

9. Mindful Communication:

- Practice being totally involved and present in the conversation; avoid distractions and multitasking while conversing.

10. Handling Conflict:

- Maintain your cool during conflicts.
- Keep your attention on the issue at hand and avoid personal attacks.
- Actively listen to the other person's point of view and collaborate to develop answers.

11. Flexibility:

- Be willing to modify your communication style to accommodate the preferences of the other person.
- Recognize that various people communicate in unique ways.

12. Giving and Receiving Feedback:

- Provide helpful and nonjudgmental feedback.
- Be open to feedback and use it to advance your career.

Keep in mind that successful communication is a talent that requires practice. It entails not only speaking but also listening, comprehending, and deliberately replying. You may strengthen your connections, handle disagreements more efficiently, and foster healthier relationships in all facets of your life by honing your communication skills.

Addressing Conflict and Misunderstandings

Addressing disagreement and misunderstandings is a necessary skill for healthy relationships and successful communication. Conflicts and misunderstandings are unavoidable in any relationship, but how you address them can make or break the partnership. Here's a step-by-step guide to dealing with conflict and resolving misunderstandings:

1. Stay Calm:

- Approach the situation with a cool and serene approach. Emotional reactions might exacerbate the argument, so take a breather before responding.

2. Choose the Right Time and Place:

- Set aside a suitable time and a discreet location to discuss the matter.
- Avoid addressing the disagreement in public or when either partner is upset or pressed for time.

3. Active Listening:

- Allow the other person to voice their point of view.
- Pay close attention without interrupting or pre-planning your response.

4. Clarify and Ask Questions:

- Ask for clarification to ensure you grasp their point of view.

- Ask open-ended inquiries to get more information about their feelings and thoughts.

5. Express Your Perspective:

- Use "I" expressions to express your thoughts and feelings.
- Avoid blaming or accusing others and instead concentrate on your own feelings and perceptions.

6. Find Common Ground:

- Search for points of agreement or shared understanding.
- Highlighting common ground might help to set a positive tone for the discussion.

7. Stay Solution-Focused:

- Instead of focusing on the problem, transfer your attention to finding a solution.
- Collaborate to explore potential solutions that address both sides' concerns.

8. Use "I" Statements:

- Avoid seeming accusatory by framing your issues with "I" phrases.
- For example, instead of "You always..." use "I felt hurt when..."

9. Avoid Escalation:

- Avoid raising your voice or using violent words; Concentrate on the problem at hand; and Avoid bringing up unrelated prior battles.

10. Apologize and Forgive:

- If you make a mistake, honestly apologize; if the other person apologizes, be open to forgiving and moving forward.

11. Seek Compromise:

- Be willing to give and take in order to establish a mutually acceptable solution. Compromise frequently entails finding a middle ground and making concessions.

12. Agree on Next Steps:

- Agree on concrete steps that both parties will take to address the conflict.
- Create a strategy for avoiding such disagreements in the future.

13. Follow Up:

- Follow up after the initial conversation to see how things are going.
- Ensure that all parties carry out their agreed-upon actions.

14. Learn and Grow:

- See disputes as chances for growth and improvement.
- Consider how you can apply what you've learnt from the event in future conversations.

Remember that dealing with disagreement and misconceptions necessitates active listening, empathy, and a willingness to collaborate in order to find a solution. You may manage challenging talks in a way that fosters relationships and promotes understanding by approaching issues with a courteous and solution-oriented perspective.

Social Anxiety and Building Social Confidence

The symptoms of social anxiety include great fear and anxiety in social situations, as well as a strong desire to avoid them. It can have a substantial impact on your capacity to interact with others, build connections, and engage in social activities. Building social confidence is a process that entails challenging your worried beliefs, practicing social skills, and gradually exposing oneself to social situations. Here's how to work on increasing your social confidence:

1. *Understand Your Anxiety:*

- Understand social anxiety and how it affects your thoughts, feelings, and behaviors.
- Recognize that social anxiety is a widespread problem that affects many people.

2. Challenge Negative Thoughts:

- Recognize and confront negative thoughts that contribute to your anxiety.
- Consider whether your opinions are supported by evidence or are overstated.

3. Practice Positive Self-Talk:

- Replace negative self-talk with positive and caring self-talk.
- Remind yourself of your strengths and encourage yourself.

4. Start Small:

- To begin, put yourself in less daunting social situations.
- As your confidence grows, gradually progress to more difficult circumstances.

5. Set Realistic Goals:

- Establish attainable goals for social interactions.
- Instead of striving for perfection, concentrate on development and improvement.

6. Focus on Listening:

- Turn your attention away from your own concern and toward what others are saying. Active listening can help you engage in more natural discussions.

7. Practice Active Listening:

- Ask questions and express genuine interest in other people's perspectives and experiences.
- Active listening encourages meaningful interactions and shifts the focus away from your anxieties.

8. Use Relaxation Techniques:

- Use relaxation techniques to handle anxiety in social situations, such as deep breathing or progressive muscle relaxation.

9. Join Supportive Groups:

- Participate in clubs, classes, or groups that are linked to your interests. Being in a supportive environment can assist ease social encounters.

10. Exposure Therapy:

- Introduce yourself gradually to social situations that cause anxiety.
- Begin with less frightening scenarios and work your way up.

11. Visualize Success:

- Visualize yourself succeeding in social situations. Visualization can help you develop a positive mentality and minimize anxiety.

12. Seek Professional Help:

- Consult with a therapist who specializes in treating social anxiety; therapy can provide specific solutions and support to help you overcome your difficulties.

13. Celebrate Small Wins:

- Recognize and appreciate your accomplishments, no matter how minor.
- Developing social confidence is a step-by-step process in which every accomplishment counts.

Keep in mind that developing social confidence requires time and perseverance. Be gentle with yourself and accept that setbacks are a normal part of the process. You can overcome social anxiety and create healthy social connections by progressively confronting your anxieties, questioning your anxious thoughts, and practicing social skills.

Chapter 8: Self-Care and Well-Being

The Role of Self-Care in Mental Health

Self-care is essential for sustaining and promoting mental health and well-being. It entails taking intentional steps to meet your physical, emotional, and psychological needs. Regular self-care routines can reduce stress, increase mood, boost resilience, and prevent burnout. Here are some of the reasons why self-care is vital for mental health:

1. Stress Reduction:

- Relaxation techniques, mindfulness, and hobbies are examples of self-care activities that can help reduce stress and promote relaxation.
- Taking breaks and engaging in fun activities can assist in reducing the harmful impact of stress on mental health.

2. Emotional Regulation:

- Self-care allows you to acknowledge and process your feelings.
- Doing things that bring you joy, comfort, or relaxation can help you control your emotions and boost your mood.

3. Prevention of Burnout:

- Regular self-care aids in the prevention of burnout, which can occur when you repeatedly disregard your own well-being.
- Prioritizing self-care ensures that you have the energy and resources to efficiently manage your duties.

4. Improved Self-Esteem:

- Taking care of yourself sends a message to yourself that you respect your own well-being.
- Practicing self-care over time can increase your self-esteem and self-worth.

5. Increased Resilience:

- Self-care promotes resilience by providing coping techniques for dealing with life's obstacles.
- Practicing self-care can improve your ability to recover from setbacks and adjust to challenges.

6. Better Boundaries:

- Self-care entails setting limits and prioritizing your needs.
- Setting and maintaining good limits can lead to more balanced and satisfying relationships.

7. Enhanced Physical Health:

- Physical health behaviors such as regular exercise, right nutrition, and adequate sleep are examples of self-care.
- Physical well-being is inextricably related to mental health, and taking care of your body can help your mind.

8. Reduced Anxiety and Depression:

- Engaging in self-care activities that promote relaxation and pleasant feelings can help relieve symptoms of anxiety and depression. Self-care can also be used to avoid these mental health issues.

9. Mindful Awareness:

- Self-care encourages you to be present and attentive of your own needs; mindfulness activities can help you handle stress and negative thoughts.

10. Personal Growth:

- Self-care is an opportunity for personal growth and self-discovery; you may improve your life experiences by attempting new activities, exploring your hobbies, and prioritizing your well-being.

It is important to remember that self-care is not a one-size-fits-all idea. It is critical to identify self-care activities that are meaningful to you and fit your tastes. Regular self-care may have a dramatic positive impact on your mental health and overall quality of life, whether it's reading, spending time in nature, practicing a hobby, or simply taking quiet minutes for yourself.

Practicing Mindfulness and Grounding Techniques

Mindfulness and grounding skills can be extremely beneficial for dealing with stress, anxiety, and overpowering emotions. These approaches assist you in remaining present, reducing rumination, and focusing your attention on the here and now. You can attempt the following mindfulness and grounding techniques:

Mindfulness Techniques:

1. *Mindful Breathing:*

- Pay attention to your breathing as you inhale and exhale.
- If your mind wanders, gently bring it back to your breathing.
- Pay attention to how your breath fills and exits your body.

2. *Body Scan:*

- Notice any sensations, tension, or relaxation in each area of your body, beginning with your toes and working your way up to your head.

3. Five Senses Exercise:

- Take note of five things that you can see, four things that you can touch, three things that you can hear, two things that you can smell, and one item that you can taste. By activating your senses, this practice helps bring you into the present moment.

4. Mindful Eating:

- Consume a little amount of food slowly and carefully.
- As you chew and swallow, pay attention to the taste, texture, and feelings.

5. Observing Your Thoughts:

- Sit quietly and observe your ideas objectively.
- Visualize your thoughts as passing clouds in the sky, acknowledging them but not getting caught up in them.

Grounding Techniques:

1. 5-4-3-2-1 Technique:

- Name five things that you can see, four things that you can touch, three things that you can hear, two things that you can smell, and one item that you can taste. This technique assists in grounding you in the present moment and reducing worry.

2. Grounding with Your Body:

- Feel your body weight in the chair or on the ground.
- Firmly press your feet into the ground and pay attention to the sensation.

3. Counting Breath:

- Slowly inhale to a count of four, then exhale to a count of four, concentrating completely on your breath and the counting.

4. Use Objects:

- Notice the texture, weight, and temperature of a small object in your hand; this draws your attention to the physical sensations in your hand.

5. Guided Imagery:

- Close your eyes and envision yourself in a peaceful and secure environment.
- Visualize the details of this location.

Mindfulness and grounding methods can be performed at any time and in any place. They help you manage stress and anxiety by shifting your focus away from troubling thoughts and into your immediate environment. With consistent use, these approaches can become valuable tools for improving your overall well-being and dealing with difficult situations.

Building a Sustainable Self-Care Routine

Creating a sustainable self-care routine is developing a series of consistent and focused actions that boost your well-being and can be sustained over time. It is about putting your physical, emotional, and mental health first by engaging in activities that nourish and renew you. Here's a step-by-step guide to developing a sustainable self-care routine:

1. Self-Reflection:

- Spend some time reflecting about your wants, hobbies, and what gives you joy and relaxation.
- Think about the areas of your life that may need more attention, such as your physical health, emotional well-being, hobbies, and relationships.

2. Set Realistic Goals:

- Begin small and create attainable self-care objectives; avoid overburdening yourself with too many activities or unrealistic expectations.

3. Prioritize Consistency:

- Developing a habit of self-care requires consistency.
- Select activities that you can realistically fit into your daily or weekly schedule.

4. Incorporate Variety:

- Include a variety of self-care activities to address various parts of your well-being; this reduces boredom and keeps your routine interesting.

5. Schedule Regularly:

- Set aside specified times each day or week for self-care activities.
- Treat these appointments as seriously as you would any other commitment.

6. Customize Your Routine:

- Create a regimen that reflects your tastes and needs.
- •What feels nurturing and delightful to you should be reflected in your self-care routine.

7. Balance Digital Detox:

- Consider implementing digital detox periods to disengage from electronics and social media;

unplugging can help you reconnect with yourself and reduce stress.

8. Practice Mindfulness:

- Incorporate mindfulness into your routine by being completely present throughout self-care tasks, which increases the benefits of the techniques you do.

9. Flexibility and Adaptability:

Be willing to adapt your routine as needed to accommodate changes in your schedule or circumstances. Adaptability ensures that your routine remains attainable.

10. Avoid Guilt:

- Prioritizing self-care is not selfish; it is necessary for your well-being. Release any guilt related with taking time for yourself.

11. Celebrate Small Wins:

- Recognize and appreciate your accomplishments, no matter how tiny; every step toward self-care is essential.

12. Review and Adjust:

- Evaluate the efficacy of your self-care practice on a regular basis.
- Make changes depending on your previous experiences and preferences.

13. Seek Professional Help:

- If you're having trouble developing a sustainable self-care regimen or are experiencing difficulties, consider obtaining help from a therapist or counselor.

Remember that self-care is a continual practice that necessitates patience and compassion for oneself. As your requirements and circumstances change, your routine may vary. The goal is to develop a self-care regimen that promotes your well-being, increases your resilience, and improves your overall quality of life.

Chapter 9: Maintaining Progress and Relapse Prevention

Strategies for Maintaining Positive Changes

Maintaining positive life changes can be difficult, but with the correct tactics and mentality, you can improve your chances of success. Here are some techniques to help you remain on track if you're working on improving your mental health, adopting healthy habits, or making other beneficial changes:

1. Set Realistic Goals:

- Establish attainable and detailed goals that are reasonable for your current situation.
- To avoid feeling overwhelmed, break down larger goals into smaller, more achievable steps.

2. Build Consistency:

- Maintaining beneficial changes requires consistency. Make your efforts a part of your daily routine.

- •Make a strategy or schedule that incorporates your new habits or routines.

3. Track Progress:

- Use a notebook, calendar, or smartphone app to keep track of your progress.
- Keep track of your accomplishments and disappointments to stay encouraged and track your progress.

4. Practice Self-Compassion:

- Be gentle with yourself and recognize that setbacks are a normal part of the process.
- Avoid self-criticism and treat yourself with the same kindness you would show a friend.

5. Celebrate Achievements:

- Rejoice in your accomplishments, no matter how minor.
- Reward yourself for achieving goals in order to encourage positive behavior.

6. Stay Mindful:

- Use mindfulness to stay present and focused on your goals. Mindfulness can help you overcome distractions and stay committed.

7. Accountability:

- Discuss your objectives with a friend, family member, or support group.
- Having someone hold you accountable might help motivate and encourage you.

8. Visualize Success:

- Use visualization tools to envision oneself effectively keeping beneficial improvements.
- Visualizing favorable results will help you stay motivated.

9. Overcome Challenges:

- Plan for potential hurdles or impediments and how you will overcome them.

- Create techniques for dealing with setbacks and remaining resilient.

10. Review and Reflect:

- Review your progress on a regular basis and reflect on the positive adjustments you've achieved. This might increase your self-esteem and remind you of the wonderful influence you're having.

11. Seek Professional Support:

- If you're having difficulty maintaining positive adjustments, consider consulting with a therapist, coach, or counselor. Professionals can develop customized plans and provide support for your individual goals.

12. Flexibility and Adaptability:

- Be willing to change your approach as needed; Because life conditions change, your solutions should be adaptable.

13. Focus on the Why:

- Recall why you began making these beneficial adjustments in the first place. Staying committed might be aided by connecting with your fundamental reasons.

14. Positive Self-Talk:

- Reinforce your efforts with positive affirmations and self-talk.
- Replace negative thoughts with statements that are powerful and supportive.

Maintaining positive changes is a journey, and setbacks are natural. The idea is to consider setbacks as chances for growth and to keep moving forward. By implementing these tactics and remaining patient and persistent, you can create long-term good improvements in your life.

Recognizing Warning Signs of Relapse

Recognizing relapse warning signs is critical for people who have made positive adjustments in their lives, especially those recovering from addiction, mental health issues, or other behavioral changes. Detecting these warning signs early allows you to take preventative measures to avoid a relapse. Here are some frequent warning indicators to be aware of:

1. Negative Mood Changes:

- Sudden mood swings, increased irritation, rage, or frequent bouts of sorrow. Persistent sensations of anxiety, restlessness, or hopelessness.

2. Isolation and Withdrawal:

- Withdrawing from friends, family, and social support.
- Isolation and avoidance of social connections.

3. Loss of Interest:

- Loss of interest in formerly enjoyable activities.
- Ignoring hobbies and activities that used to give you pleasure.

4. Increased Stress:

- Excessive stress or difficulties dealing with pressures.
- A sense that you are losing control of your emotions.

5. Neglecting Self-Care:

- Neglecting self-care activities including exercise, good diet, and sleep.
- Forgetting about personal hygiene and grooming procedures.

6. Cravings and Urges:

- Strong desires or urges to engage in the activities you were attempting to change.
- Feeling on the verge of reverting to previous habits.

7. Obsessive Thinking:

- Obsessive thoughts about the conduct that you were attempting to avoid.
- Constantly thinking about the substances or habits you've been attempting to avoid.

8. Changes in Sleeping and Eating Patterns:

- Sleep disturbances such as insomnia or oversleeping.
- Significant changes in appetite that result in weight loss or gain.

9. Rationalization and Minimization:

- Justifying and reasoning the reasons for resuming old habits.
- Reducing the negative effects of participating in the behavior.

10. Increased Secretive Behavior:

- Increasing your secrecy regarding your acts or location.
- Feeling compelled to conceal certain activities from others.

11. Decline in Performance:

- A significant reduction in job, school, or personal duties.
- Difficulty focusing and being productive.

12. Loss of Motivation:

- A lack of passion and motivation for your goals and beneficial improvements.
- Having difficulty finding meaning or purpose in your endeavors.

13. Reconnecting with Triggers:

- Reconnecting with people, places, or situations related to the behavior you were attempting to modify.
- Putting oneself in triggering situations.

14. Resuming Old Habits:

- Giving in to your impulses and indulging in the activity you were attempting to avoid.
- Despite past attempts, returning to old routines.

15. Denial:

- Denying or downplaying warning indicators that you are at risk of relapse.
- Ignoring comments from family members or professionals.

It is crucial to highlight that relapse is a normal part of the recovery process, and understanding warning signs does not guarantee relapse. If you detect these symptoms in yourself or someone you care about, it is critical that you seek help and take action to avoid a full relapse. Contact your support network, therapist, counselor, or treatment provider for advice and assistance in dealing with these difficulties.

Creating a Personalized Relapse Prevention Plan

Developing a specific relapse prevention strategy is a proactive method to protecting the gains you've made in beneficial changes, such as recovering addiction, managing mental health, or any other behavioral change. This strategy will assist you in identifying potential triggers, warning signals, and coping skills to help you avoid a relapse. Here's how to make your own relapse prevention plan:

1. *Identify Your Triggers:*

- Make a list of scenarios, people, locations, and feelings that could set off the unwanted behavior.
- Be explicit and thorough when identifying potential triggers.

2. Recognize Warning Signs:

- Consider the warning signs you've seen in the past that indicate you're at danger of relapse, such as changes in mood, behavior, thoughts, or feelings.

3. Develop Coping Strategies:

- Make a list of healthy coping methods to utilize when confronted with triggers or warning flags.
- Incorporate tactics like as deep breathing, mindfulness, chatting to a friend, doing a pastime, or getting expert help.

4. Create an Emergency Plan:

- Create a plan for what to do if you find yourself in a high-risk position or experiencing overwhelming desires.

- Determine precise steps you may take to withdraw yourself from the situation or seek emergency assistance.

5. Utilize Support Network:

- Make a list of people you can turn to for help when you're feeling down. Friends, family, support groups, therapists, or mentors could all be included.

6. Practice Self-Care:

- Include in your plan self-care activities that support your physical, emotional, and mental well-being.
- Self-care relieves stress and prevents triggers from becoming overpowering.

7. Set Realistic Goals:

- Set short-term and long-term goals for your beneficial changes.
- To offer a sense of accomplishment, break these goals down into manageable steps.

8. Stay Mindful:

- Include mindfulness practices in your strategy to help you stay present and moderate your urges.
- Mindfulness can help you respond to triggers rather than react to them.

9. Review Your Plan Regularly:

- Review and update your relapse prevention strategy on a regular basis; when circumstances change, alter your methods and triggers accordingly.

10. Visualize Success:

- Visualize yourself successfully navigating difficult situations without succumbing to the behavior you want to avoid. Positive visualization helps reinforce your commitment.

11. Practice Self-Compassion:

- Be gentle with yourself if you have setbacks.

- Recognize that relapse is a normal part of the process and that it is an opportunity to learn and improve.

12. Seek Professional Help:

- Seek advice from a therapist, counselor, or treatment provider if you're unsure how to construct a relapse prevention strategy. Professionals can assist you in developing a plan that is tailored to your individual requirements.

Creating a customized relapse prevention plan allows you to take control of your path and equips you with coping methods. Remember that your plan is a living document that will change as you progress and gain experience. It serves as a reminder that you have the abilities and resources to sustain the beneficial improvements you've worked so hard to attain.

Chapter 10: Your Unbreakable Future

Reflecting on Your CBT Journey

Reflecting on your Cognitive Behavioral Therapy (CBT) experience can be a beneficial exercise for assessing your development, identifying progress, and gaining insights into your thoughts and behaviors. Reflecting on your journey can help you understand the changes you've made and how they've impacted your well-being because CBT is a structured technique that focuses on modifying harmful thought patterns and behaviors. Here are some suggestions to help you reflect on your CBT experience:

1. Review Your Goals:

- Remember the goals you set at the start of your CBT adventure. These could be connected to anxiety management, mood improvement, or modifying certain behaviors.

2. Document Progress:

- Make a list of the changes in your thoughts, feelings, and actions that you've noticed since beginning CBT.
- Take note of any improvements in negative thinking management, coping with challenges, or engaging in good actions.

3. Recognize Patterns:

- List any patterns or triggers you've identified through CBT.
- Recognize how specific situations or thoughts influence your emotions and behaviour.

4. Challenge Negative Thoughts:

- Consider how you've learnt to question and reframe negative or skewed views.
- Think about particular situations where you were able to shift your perspective.

5. Identify Coping Strategies:

- Make a list of the coping methods and practices you've learnt through CBT.

- Consider how these tactics have helped you deal with stress, anxiety, or other difficulties.

6. Celebrate Achievements:

- Recognize your accomplishments, no matter how minor.
- Recognize the strides you've made in managing your mental health.

7. Evaluate Challenges:

- Consider the difficulties you encountered along your CBT journey.
- Consider how you overcome challenges and what you gained from them.

8. Assess Behavioral Changes:

- Consider any behavioral modifications that match with your CBT aims.
- Have you been able to form new habits or respond differently in different situations?

9. Explore Relapses:

- If you had setbacks or relapses, consider what caused them.
- Think about how you can use the skills you've acquired to avoid future relapses.

10. Future Planning:

- Consider how you can continue to implement CBT ideas in your daily life.
- Consider how you will sustain your progress and continue practicing the strategies.

11. Gratitude and Self-Compassion:

- Express your appreciation for the time and effort you've invested into your CBT journey.
- Be patient with yourself, understanding that improvement requires time and work.

12. Seek Support:

- Discuss your reflections with your therapist or counselor during your appointments; they may provide guidance, comments, and help you plan for the future.

Reflection allows you to consolidate your learning and implement CBT skills into your daily life. It's an opportunity to celebrate your accomplishments, learn from your struggles, and continue to lay a solid foundation for your mental health.

Applying CBT Principles Beyond the Book

Applying Cognitive Behavioral Therapy (CBT) principles outside of the therapeutic context can significantly improve your capacity to manage your thoughts, emotions, and behaviors in daily life. While engaging with a therapist is beneficial, incorporating CBT ideas into your everyday routine allows you to continue using effective tactics to improve your mental health. Here are some examples of how you can apply CBT ideas outside of the book:

1. Mindfulness and Awareness:

- Use mindfulness techniques to stay present and aware of your thoughts and feelings.
- Pay attention to negative thought patterns and utilize CBT strategies to confront and reframe them.

2. Thought Monitoring:

- Constantly scrutinize your thoughts for negative or skewed patterns.
- Keep a journal or use a note-taking software to keep track of your thoughts and identify recurrent themes.

3. Cognitive Restructuring:

- Whenever you notice negative thoughts, apply cognitive restructuring techniques to challenge and reframe them.
- Replace irrational beliefs with more balanced and evidence-based perspectives.

4. Behavior Analysis:

- Examine your habits and their triggers to spot patterns. This can assist you in understanding the connection between your thoughts, emotions, and actions.

5. Exposure Therapy:

- Gradually expose yourself to situations that make you anxious or uncomfortable.
- Apply what you've learned to handle and cope with real-life situations.

6. Behavioral Activation:

- Participate in activities that provide you joy and a sense of accomplishment.
- Make a plan that includes pleasurable and important activities that will lift your spirits.

7. Self-Care and Stress Management:

- Prioritize CBT-aligned self-care strategies such as relaxation techniques, physical activity, and healthy routines.

8. Goal Setting:

- Establish realistic and attainable goals that correspond to the desired improvements.
- Divide larger goals into smaller, more manageable tasks.

9. Reframing Cognitive Distortions:

- Constantly question cognitive distortions such as black-and-white thinking, catastrophizing, and personalizing, and reframe them with more balanced and realistic perspectives.

10. Self-Talk and Positive Affirmations:

- Monitor your inner dialogue and replace self-criticism with self-compassion.
- Use positive affirmations to counteract negative thinking and increase self-esteem.

11. Problem-Solving Skills:

- Use problem-solving strategies to overcome obstacles and make sound decisions.
- Break down challenges into manageable components and investigate viable solutions.

12. Social Skills:

- In your relationships with others, use effective communication, active listening, and empathy.
- Make use of your social talents to form healthy relationships and resolve issues.

13. Relapse Prevention:

- Review and adapt your relapse prevention plan on a regular basis.
- Remain diligent in spotting warning signals and using relapse prevention techniques.

14. Self-Evaluation and Reflection:

- Reflect on your progress and the use of CBT principles in your life on a regular basis.

- Recognize your accomplishments and highlight areas where you may improve.

Keep in mind that applying CBT principles necessitates continual effort and practice. As you incorporate these approaches into your daily life, you will lay a solid foundation for managing your mental health and making long-term good changes. If you find it difficult to do this on your own, think about getting continuous help from a therapist or counselor.

Made in the USA
Monee, IL
21 November 2023